YOUR KNOWLEDGE HAS VALUE

- We will publish your bachelor's and
  master's thesis, essays and papers

- Your own eBook and book -
  sold worldwide in all relevant shops

- Earn money with each sale

Upload your text at www.GRIN.com
and publish for free

Arif Hakim

A discussion on the article 'Generalised improvement in speech production for subject with reproduction conduction aphasia'

GRIN Verlag

Bibliografische Information der Deutschen Nationalbibliothek:

Die Deutsche Bibliothek verzeichnet diese Publikation in der Deutschen National-
bibliografie; detaillierte bibliografische Daten sind im Internet über http://dnb.d-
nb.de/ abrufbar.

Imprint:

Copyright © 2006 GRIN Verlag GmbH
Druck und Bindung: Books on Demand GmbH, Norderstedt Germany
ISBN: 978-3-656-40862-8

A discussion on the article *'Generalised improvement in speech production for subject with reproduction conduction aphasia'* written by Sue Franklin, Frauke Buerk, and David Howard.

Hakim Arif

Introduction

Speech production, the prime language activity of human beings, involves a process of cognitive endowment. It includes some internal mechanism of language production that engages several chronological stages like auditory analysis system, phonological input lexicon, phonological output lexicon, and output buffer. Here, impairments in former two stages exhibit comprehension problems of speech production of human beings, whereas impairments in later two stages denote production deficiency in this regard (Basso, 2003: 127). In the article *'Generalised improvement in speech production for subject with reproduction conduction aphasia'* Sue Franklin, Frauke Buerk, and David Howard depicted a case study of a patient MB who faced a problem with speech production especially phonological encoding process at the post lexical level that includes phonological output lexicon and output buffer. Thus, MB made frequent phonological production errors in all modalities but reduced significantly after some therapy sessions conducted by the authors of the article.

MB, a retired 83-years old widow with several children as well as grandchildren, was suffering a left middle cerebral artery infraction due to transient ischaemic attacks. Finally such an infraction of MB turned into a specific form of aphasia named 'reproduction conduction aphasia'. Shallice and Warrington (1977) mentioned phonological impairment in production with good comprehension as the main characteristics of reproduction conduction aphasia. Thus, it assumed also to be continued to MB in terns of production difficulty in phonology. Hence, in order to identify such typical reproduction conduction aphasia, symptom of MB, the authors of this article conducted several intervention processes. They were also motivated by some pioneering research activities in the domain of cognitive neuropsychology that could be mentioned here briefly.

Previous literature

Levelt et al (1999) proposed a speech production model containing functionally separable levels of lexical semantic representation, phonological semantic representation and phonological encoding. According to this model, information is processed serially so that only one output is fed forward from each processing level to the next. Here, phonological lexical deficit should therefore sensitive to word frequency and would affect naming, but not repetition. In addition, deficit of phonological encoding would not result in a word frequency effect, but all output modalities would be affected.

Dell et al (1997) proposed a different model of speech production that contains three layers corresponding to semantic feature nodes, lexical nodes, and phonemes. In their model they did not consider word frequency effect, but emphasized on connection from lexical level to phoneme level and from phoneme level to lexical level and are equal in their connection strength. If this method is applied irrespective of word phoneme length, longer word would benefit because of more feedback from the richer representation at the phoneme level, and it would tend a result in a greater probability to correct lexical item with longer words. Because longer words require more phonemes to be correctly activated, thus, difficulty in phoneme selection would result in poor performance in longer words.

Miller & Ellis (1987) proposed the concept of rapid decay of phonological representation. According to them, during the processing of phonological assembly in the case of reproduction conduction aphasia the phonological errors in production are rapid decay of phonological representation. This model explained the tendency for more errors with longer words and suggested that phonological errors should occur towards the end of words.

Caramazza et al (1986) reported patients with intact repetition and oral reading for real words and impaired repetition and oral reading for non words. Thus, they provided the concept of a strong dissociation between word and non-word production and suggested difference of phonological encoding of real and non-words

Monitoring accounts, an alternative account of phonological errors in speech production by Sehlenk et al (1987), assumed that fluent and correctly formed speech is only achieved by covert repairs being carried out in response to a constant monitoring of the output. And if there is impairment in *'inner speech'*, there would be phonologically disordered speech.

A phonological encoding model proposed by Levelt et al (1999) begins with the point of lexical retrieval. Here, phoneme segment and the metrical information are processed in parallel. The phoneme segment, then, are inserted into a frame which is used to form syllable.

Baseline test

As a baseline test MB was given the *Nickels Naming Test* on two occasions 1 month apart with a view to knowing whether spontaneous recovery was occurring. Written sentence comprehension using TROG was assessed in the same two occasions where she made errors in the second half of the study and exhibited a sentence level deficit. This written sentence comprehension was used as a control task throughout the therapy as no improvement would be expected on written sentence comprehension.

Pre-Assessments Tasks

With a view to identifying the nature of phonological errors of MB in all modalities the authors conducted some pre-assessments and consequently post treatments. These were mainly performed to be informed about the nature and characteristics of existing phonological errors of MB. Pre-assessment stage includes some important tasks e.g. *Spoken word-to-picture matching, Auditory Matching Span,* and *Auditory rhyme judgements* with a view to assessing MB's auditory input processing system. Her performance was as good as normal people in the former two tasks; especially in *Auditory Matching Span* she was able to compare string of six digits correctly. But in the *auditory rhyme judgements* task MB's performance was better than chance but very poor and indicated her abnormally slow responses in the integrity of the input phonological system as well as segmentation skills.

The *Nickels' naming test* was also used in the pre-assessment stage in order to assess MB's naming and oral repetition and reading, and non-word repetition and reading. But she performed poorly in all modalities and produced phonemic errors including omissions, substitutions and errors of repeated attempts conforming to the level *'conduite d' approache'*. In the assessment of non-word repetition and reading MB showed greater difficulty with non-words than real words and there was a significant effect of syllable length for oral reading of non-words, but not in repetition.

In addition, there was a task of connected speech in the pre-assessment stage where she was asked to re-tell the story of Cinderella. In this task, MB performed poorly and produced neologisms and phonological paraphasias.

Summary of the pre-assessments tasks mainly indicated MB's phonological errors identified by word length and characterised by phonological searching and *'conduite d' approache'*. In addition, there existed auditory processing problems in auditory rhyme judgements task of MB. Thus, the authors hypothesized that MB had post lexical, phonological output problem.

Tests of treatment

Having gotten the result of pre-assessment tasks, the authors designed the tests for MB containing following five phases:

1. *First pre-test*: Contained naming of the 130 items in *Nickels' naming test* and divided randomly into two sets— numbers of phoneme clusters and numbers of syllables where set was used as treatment item and other as control set. She was also tested in repetition and reading of a set of 26 low-imageability words in addition to the 130-items for naming. In order to assess MB's spontaneous speech production, she was asked to tell the story of Cinderella.

2. *Second pre-test*: 130-items and written TORG were represented to know the improvement of the naming test and TORG.

3. *After the first phase of therapy*: Contained *Nickels' naming test* and a test of picture naming in sentences. MB had to present a composite picture developed from naming test and asked to describe it.

4. *After the end of second phase of therapy*: 130-items from *Nickels' naming test* were used by MB in the test of naming, repetition, reading and naming in sentence. In addition, 65 non-words were presented to evaluate the improvement with non-words reading of MB. She was also asked to re-tell the Cinderella story to know her change in spontaneous speech.

5. *Follow up*: 130-items naming were also tested by MB after four months of first treatment to see whether the therapy was continued.

Treatments

Treatments were carried out in 5 phases. Among these, first two were related to comprehension tasks, whereas the last three were concerned with MB's speech production ability.

Phase 1: Phoneme discrimination tasks aimed at the early auditory processing stages of MB. In the first two sessions MB corrected 90% and 94% of total items. End of the next two sessions concerning listening to the ends of the words she corrected 95% items.

Phase 2: This self-monitoring phase consisted of three successive stages with increasing task complexity. Each session used 20 words from the treatment set of 65 items and lasted 30 minutes.

Phase 2a: In this 'external monitoring' phase MB had to judge whether the word was correct or incorrect including identifying location of the errors.

Phase 2b: This 'indirect monitoring' phase insured MB's response in naming the picture from treatment test.

Phase 2c: In this 'direct internal monitoring' or 'on-line judgement' phase MB was given a picture and asked to produce the correct word for the picture and later she was asked to build a sentence.

The overall result of this study showed that the therapy was successful and MB had significant improvement in all output modalities following treatments. MB showed reduced *'conduite d' approache'* errors during therapy session. Treatment for naming, oral reading of word, word repetition and naming in sentence exhibited significant improvement, though none of these fields mentioned did differ significantly with control task. But though the number of non-words reading correctly had not changed following therapy, significantly more phonemes were produced correctly. In addition, there was an approach to generalize the result of treatments to words not used in the therapy.

Further Analysis

The result of treatments also helped provide some further analysis concerning phonological output deficit of MB. She had post-lexical deficit than lexical. Because MB neither exhibited word frequency effect, the main characteristics of lexical deficit, at any modalities, nor showed the effect of imageability and the number of syllables in the target. Rather the number of phonemes in the word affected her performance in all output tasks. In addition, her speech production was worse for non-words than real words, though there was a significant improvement in oral reading of non-words following treatment. Thus, both the deficit and improvement occurred in post-lexical level.

As MB's accuracy in word production was determined by the number of phonemes rather than syllables in all output modalities, she had a deficit at the level of phoneme. In fact, she exhibited two different types of phoneme deficiencies in her speech production. The more phonemes are in the word, the greater probability of errors, if the system worked noisily or inefficiently. Errors, on the other hand, occurred towards end of the word, if phoneme encoding could be affected by abnormally fast decay.

Data of MB's performance regarding speech production is supported by the decay theory. According to the left-to-right model of this theory depicted by Miller and Ellis (1987), errors should be more frequent at the longer word as well as at the end of the word. MB performed more errors at every position of longer word compared to shorter words, and produced more number of errors later in the word. She abandoned words that were incorrect during or after the first or second syllable indicated that errors in later words tended to be omissions rather than substitutions. During two naming pre-tests MB's omission errors occurred in the later syllable, whereas substitution errors did not show any effect of word position. But After therapy, the number of omission errors almost unchanged but the number of substitution errors showed an equal decrease across all syllable positions.

Some common observation

The result of both pre-assessment tasks and post-treatments conducted by the authors in order to elicit the nature of speech production of MB helped them make some common observations that could be mentioned in the following.

- MB was impaired with a post-lexical deficit in phonological encoding.
- She made phonological errors in reading, repetition and naming.
- Her repeated self-correcting attempts at producing a word *(conduite d' approche)* were often successful.
- MB had no short term memory deficit, because she was able to match string of digit up to six items long.
- She had no semantic impairment that could create difficulty in production.
- She made no semantic errors in picture naming than control subjects.

- Phoneme length affected word production in all output modalities.
- MB was worse at producing non-words than real words and both these types of words showed a similar qualitative impairment in terms of errors type and length.
- Her words and non-words impairment were consistent with the notion of one-way dissociation.
- The therapy carried out with MB had developed her ability to monitor own speech production.
- Both before and after therapy *conduite d' approache* demonstrated excellent ability to produce self-correction. It indicated her intact lexical processing.
- Therapy was successful both in the amount of improvement and in its generalisation across items and tasks.

Some comments

This is a pioneering research article in the field of the therapy of aphasia especially reproduction conduction aphasia that elicited the nature of deficiency in concerned field. The authors of this article tried to introduce some fundamental approaches to the therapy of reproduction conduction aphasia. Though the treatment processes were applied to extract the nature of speech production of one patient, but the result indicated that the methods and treatments followed could be advocated to the needs of patients. Because the treatments used in this experiment were successful and the patient improved significantly in all modalities.

But, the authors conducted a lot of pre-assessments tasks and post-treatments in order to identify as well as to make cure the sole phonological deficit of MB. In addition, there also exist overlapping in the description concerning implementation of assessments and treatment especially during the depiction of phases of treatments. Finally, as MB performed worse in non-words reading and repetition, we can predict that her sublexical route is severely damaged (Basso, 2003; Edmundson, 1995; Hillis, 2000). But the authors did not mention this at any rate.

References

Basso, Anna (2003). *Aphasia and its Therapy*. Oxford University Press

Caramazza, A., Miceli, G., & Villa, G.(1986). The role of the (output) phonological buffer in reading, writing and repetition. *Cognitive psychology 3,* 37-76

Dell, G.S., Schwartz, M.F., Martin, N., Saffran, E.M., & Gagnon D.A.(1997). Lexical access in aphasic and nonaphasic speakers. *Psychology Review*, 104, 801-838

Edmundson, A., and McIntosh, J.(1995). Cognitive Neuropsychology and Aphasia Therapy: Putting the Theory into Practice. In Chris Code and Dave Muller(eds.) *The Treatment of Aphasia: From Theory to Practice,* 137-163. Singular Publishing Group, Inc. San Diego, California

Hillis, Argye E.(2000). The Organization of Lexical System. In Brenda Rapp(ed.) *The Handbook of Cognitive Neuropsychology What Deficits Reveal About the Human Mind.* 185-210. Psychology Press

Levelt, W.J.M., Roelofs, A., & Meyer, A.S.(1999). A theory of Lexical access in speech production. *Behavioural and Brain Science,* 22, 1-25

Miller, D., & Ellis, A.W.(1987). Speech and writing errors in 'neologistic jargonaphasia': A lexical activation hypothesis. In M. Coltheart, R. Job, & G, Sartori (Eds.), *The Cognitive Neuropsychology of Language.* Hove, UK

Schlenk, K-J., Huber, W., & Willmes, K.(1987). 'Prepairs' and repairs. Different monitoring functions in aphasic language production. *Brain and Language*, 30, 226-244

Shallice, T., and Warrington, E.K(1977). Auditory-verbal and short-term memory impairment and conduction aphasia. *Brain and Language, 4.* 479-491